How To Meet Fairies

Sheila Jeffries

www.capallbann.co.uk

How To Meet Fairies

©2001 Sheila Jeffries

ISBN 186163 1499

Cover design by Paul Mason

Published by:

Capall Bann Publishing
Freshfields
Chieveley
Berks
RG20 8TF

Dedication

The love and support of my friends is something I deeply treasure, so this book is dedicated to them.

Table of Contents

'O let us talk of quiet that we know,
that we can know, the deep and lovely
quiet of a strong heart at peace.'

D.H. Lawrence

Chapter 1

Mysterious Beings of Light

Tomby

Being a Swan

Journey inside a Crystal

The Rose Pink City

The Microcosm

Chapter 1
Mysterious Beings of Light

Tomby

My first encounter with a nature spirit was in my home garden at the age of three. It was shown to me by a friend.

'Look!' she called 'A gnome!'

'Where?'

'Going into the wall. He's like a little green light.'

In a gloomy part of the garden the emerald light was hypnotic. It was the size of an upright housebrick, moving along the ground. It glided into a hole between two blocks of the blue-lias stone peculiar to the Glastonbury area. Purple toadflax, yellow stonecrop and zig zags of ivy covered the old wall. We pressed our faces to the hole, smelling moss and feeling prickly lichen on our cheeks, and we could still see the green luminescence inside.

Daily observation of the comings and goings revealed that the emerald light had a definite routine, emerging at the hours of nine, twelve, three and six. It would tour the garden, always visiting the same places. Round and round the well, under the lilac bushes, through the wicket gate to disappear into the leafy roots of elm trees which stood sock deep in grass. It carefully avoided our fluffy black cat who was obviously able to see it. Her golden eyes followed the light across the garden, and she crouched low, maintaining a respectful distance in its presence.

The light moved sedately, always upright, but on one occasion it burst out of the wall at a blue tit who was investigating the hole.

'This is MY place. Get out'

The message was clear, and the brilliance of the light was pulsating in an agitated way.

My concern at the unusual behaviour of the little green light must have conveyed itself, for it shot towards my favourite sitting place, a sun- warmed stone against the wall. It stood close apparently seeking protection, perhaps fearing retaliation from the blue tit.

In this breath-holding opportunity there was a chance to study the mysterious green light which shone so brightly. Right inside, small as a cat within its fluff, was a pea-green gnome with perfect features - pin-head eyes under surprised brows, a nodule of a nose and smiling cheeks. He wore lime green clothes, leggings, a jacket and a hat, and the bottle green stitching was visible in that moment as if through a magnifying glass. Every detail was clear, the crinkled knuckles, the tightly laced boots with stitches radiating round the eyelets. In one hand he carried a scroll the size of a match stick, and the whole gnome was transparent.

This tiny being looked directly into my eyes, giving out a feeling of merriment and love. Then he waved to me and instantly the green light blazed brighter, hiding him as he glided back to his hole. Had he deliberately shown himself to me?

'Who are you?' I asked aloud.

'Tomby.'

The voice came out of the wall and that was the only word I ever heard him speak.

Tomby was friendly. He stayed for years, even moving house with us and finding another hole in another blue - lias wall, and a new garden to explore.

As a child growing up in rural Somerset, I saw fairies frequently, and thought they were normal.But peer influence, the church, the family and school taught me, painfully, to repress my ability, or at least to shut up about it! Years of being a school teacher and having to be professional ensured that seeing fairies was no longer an acceptable part of life. So successful was the repression that I actually stopped seeing them. The light that had blazed such colours into my childhood world faded to a feeble glimmer.

Most of us live our lives like icebergs, with only one third of our consciousness functional, the remaining two thirds submerged under the dark waters of orthodoxy.

After years of teaching in London, I moved back to Somerset, and became further entrenched by the three bed semi and the family. Until one hot July day, in a garden on the slopes of Glastonbury Tor, I regained those long repressed abilities in one mind boggling afternoon.

Being A Swan

'You must come to tea.'

My flamboyant friend Lara had bewitched me with her knowing eyes. If she had said 'Come to tea and I'll teach you to meditate,' I would never have agreed to go! But tea sounded harmless enough. Lara was into everything I'd never allowed myself to do. Astrology, crystals, healing, past-life therapy and other esoteric goodies. We had tea in her garden complete with wind-chimes and Bhuddas. There was no polite conversation about weather and families. I expressed an interest in the crystal workshops she was running, and halfway down my cup of tea she was teaching me to meditate.

Lara taught me the heart meditation, how to sit with eyes closed and visualize a bright star coming into your heart. It was easy and soon I was having incredible visions there in Lara's garden. Another world opened before me, a vista of loving peace where abundant landscapes glowed invitingly, a world where spirit people lived. It reawakened my clairvoyance, repressed since childhood. I felt like the Ugly Duckling discovering he was a swan.

Meditation was just the beginning. In the coming months I progressed through Lara's workshops, learning how to heal, re-living past lives, working with sound, colour and crystals. All of it was life-changing.

If meditation were taught in schools there would be no need for drug-taking, no need to get drunk and seek oblivion or light a cigarette for tranquillity. What Lara had given me that day was a priceless gift that changed my life forever.

Soon after learning to meditate, I attended a workshop on crystal healing and at last the fairy kingdom was revealed to me again.

Jouɾney Insíðe A Cɾystal

The fluorite crystal shone in the palm of my hand. Against the light its deep purple reflected cornflower colours, pinks and blues, and a glint of gold. The shape was octahedral, eight triangular facets forming pyramids which ever way it was turned. Fluorite breaks naturally into these perfect geometric solids, and its natural colour can be violet, green, gold, or clear.

Here It was, on my first ever crystal workshop, not knowing what on earth to expect.

After spending a few minutes looking at the crystal we had chosen, we were asked to dedicate it to the love and light of Christ. (The word crystal is CHRIST-ALL) - Then we closed our eyes and kept still, holding our crystals. Peaceful music was played, of harp and flute mingled with sounds of running water and birdsong, with no regular beat or tune to distract us.

Going inside the crystal was easy. Size has nothing to do with it. Your spirit is measureless.

The Rose Pínk Cíty

I found myself sitting on the square inner floor of the fluorite crystal, the glassy pyramid above me, and a similar one below. The first impression was of PROTECTION and the second of WONDER. I stood up and walked in the violet light through crystal rooms and up curving flights of silver stairs. At the apex of the pyramid, I stopped and stretched up my arms feeling amazingly sylph-like and free. I was wearing a ROBE of heather pink, it was full of light and I weighed nothing!

In complete trust I opened my heart and invited LOVE to come in. The apex of the pyramid blazed and cones of light beamed down, dazzling white searchlights probing deep into the crystal. I turned and glided down the silver staircase with a sense of joy and reverence. As the light was leading me downwards it was splitting into colour rays. I first explored the pink ray of LOVE, a city of rose and lilac, of spires, domes and archways leading into perfumed gardens. I entered a healing temple of amethyst and gold, lay on a couch and allowed golden light to stream down on me for a long long time. I knew that God was there shining straight into the heart of the crystal, healing and energising.

The Microcosm

The light led me through a microcosm of Planet Earth, the rocks and minerals, the energy of salt and ocean, the silver arteries of water within the earth, the massive swirls of wind and rain, encapsulated like a painting inside a dome, all lit by moving shafts of light.

The emerald ray took me into the plant kingdom and there were thousands of industrious creatures working in every cell of plant life. The fairies! Minute beings of light, sparkles of the life force, busy nurturing and energising. Down and down I walked to secluded pools overhung with ferns and mosses, each one closer to the heartbeat of the earth. Greens darkened, and still light glinted into these depths. Out of the light came a voice and it said 'Even in the depths of dark you shall be protected.'

I moved upward, floating now, through rich cornfields and gardens, past a layer of resplendent insects which shone like Christmas decorations. Birds appeared, from humming birds to swans. In the centre, leading me home, was the white dove, its wings fanned out covering the sky like rays of light.The dove became the light, and I followed it home to the heart of the crystal.

Opening my eyes after this experience was such a shock. There were my feet and legs looking so cumbersome in jeans and trainers! And the colours of chairs and carpet looked grossly sludgy compared to the ethereal colours within the crystal. Somehow, inside that crystal I had re-visited the fairy kingdom and returned, healed by its radiance.

'Our birth is but a sleep and a forgetting
The Soul that rises with us, our life's Star,
Hath had elsewhere its setting
And cometh from afar.'

William Wordsworth

Chapter 2

You Have Only To Remember

Trying to be Human

Alan's Experience - The Flower of Love

Annie's Experience - Cherry Bark Fairies

How you can learn to see the Fairies

Chapter 2

You Have Only To Remember

Trying To Be Human

'We are not human beings trying to be spiritual but spirit beings trying to be human.'

Before you were conceived you were a free and joyous soul, a glorious being of light and love. Coping with finding yourself trapped inside the body of a baby is one of the greatest challenges the soul must face.

Rudolph Steiner believed that until the age of three, a child is still in the angelic realms. All small children can see nature spirits and communicate by thought telepathy. By the age of seven most have sadly learned to repress this ability because of the influence of peers, family, and school.

Everyone is given a spiritual message in early childhood, and most of us instantly forget it.The subconscious files it away in a storehouse of experiences designed to guide and nurture us through our lives. Just as our dreams sometimes elude us when we try to remember them, so our spiritual message disappears mysteriously.

But you can learn to recall it. Months after learning to meditate and practising it regularly, I attended a personal growth workshop. Before going into meditation, we were told to ask if we could be allowed to remember our spirit message, given in childhood. All of us did, and we were a widely mixed group, male and female, aged from 18 to 80, and including a few cynics!

It is the experience of one of these cynics that I share with you now.

Alan's Experience - The Flower Of Love

A successful business man in his fifties, Alan had come to the workshops because, despite his wealth, he felt his life lacked purpose. Openly sceptical, he had remained stone-faced through two previous workshops, yet he kept coming back.

On this occasion everyone emerged from meditation to find Alan beaming like a Halloween pumpkin. Tears were running down his cheeks.

'I've had the most amazing experience,' he kept saying. 'It's changed my life.'

Alan had relived a time in his childhood when he had walked into an orchard in winter, under ancient apple trees.The grass was stiff and sparkling, the ground latticed with needles of ice. Shining mist filled the air.

In this frozen world he remembered standing under an apple tree, clasping his hands in woollen gloves. And out of the frosted grass, an orange flower grew in front of his eyes, a lily filled with fire and open to the sky. A voice had spoken to Alan from the centre of the flower.

'I am the flower of love, the orange flower of the frost that blooms in this orchard, a flower that blooms no matter what, in the harshest conditions, in a hostile world, a flower that shines with holy fire, fire of me, of my spirit, spirit of love. I will never leave you.'

Alan felt God had spoken to him from within the flower, and thousands of moving sparks had surrounded him at the time. He had carefully carried some indoors to show his mother and her response was 'Don't be so stupid.'

Annie's Experience - Cherry Bark Fairies

Another person on the workshop, Annie, a twenty five year old girl whose life, in her own words, was completely messed up and hopeless, remembered the fairies coming to help her.

Annie had spent her sixth birthday in hospital recovering from whooping cough. On that balmy day in May, she had wandered out into the hospital ground in her nightie. Without being noticed she followed a winding path and came to what seemed a magical place under the sunlit branches of a flowering cherry. Annie had laid on her back gazing at flakes of sky through clustered pink blossoms. She remembered thinking that the flowers were in the sky, when she was seized by a terrible coughing fit.

Annie cried out for the nurses who normally came running to help her, but no one heard.Terrified by the paroxysms of gasping, retching cough, Annie recalled hearing a persistent voice speaking to her.

'Go to sleep Annie. Go to sleep.'

But Annie stayed awake.

She was surrounded by rose coloured fairies, their faces and clothes glowed bright as a sunset. About twenty of them crowded around her throat, holding her in loving arms. Annie felt an extraordinary sense of glistening stardust going in through her skin.

While it was happening she gazed into the eyes of one of the fairies who told her they were using the energy of cherry bark to heal the cough.The fairy explained how the vibration of the cherry tree was being used to re-tune Annie's whole being to make her body strong and shining, so that the whooping cough could no longer live in it. The fairy referred to it as 'the demon cough' and said it would leave in three days.

The cough subsided and Annie was able to walk back to her bed. She had no more coughing fits and was discharged in three days.The doctors and nurses kept expressing astonishment at her rosy face, her appetite and her energy.

Annie believes she was led to the cherry tree that day and was healed by the fairies. Remembering her experience helped her to sort her life out. She later became a qualified homeopath.

How You Can Learn To See The Fairies

You can re-discover your own spiritual message, given to you in childhood, or your early encounters with fairies. Prepare a quiet place and time to sit, make sure you are comfortable and not likely to be disturbed. Have a pen and writing pad beside you.Lighting a candle, placing flowers or a favourite crystal nearby are helpful.

Close your eyes and focus attention on your heart. Send out the request to remember your spiritual message - you can speak it aloud, or just think it.Then ask these questions, accepting that the answer will come not in words but in pictures.As soon as you have an image, build on it, filling in the details as if you were painting. Just one question may be enough to bring the whole experience to mind.

Where were you? How old were you? What were you wearing? Who was with you? What time of year was it? What time of day?

If you cannot get answers, break the questions down, for example. 'Where were you?' can be approached by asking 'Were you inside or outside?' 'Was it light or dark?' Each time phrase it so as to give only two possible choices.The right one always comes to you first, from the heart. Dithering over choices means you need to by pass your reasoning mind and re-focus on the heart. Doing this process with a like-minded friend can be helpful, with one asking the questions.

Record your experience immediately, taking time to fill in details which will undoubtedly emerge as you write, or speak into a tape recorder. Keep it forever, for this is an important part of the jigsaw of your life, and one day it will fit into place. Mine did, as you will find out when you read the chapter on Fairies and Ley Lines.

You had the ability to see fairies once, and you can learn to do it again. If you want to see fairies in your life today, here are a few things you can try. Remember you will have a better chance of seeing fairies in an unspoilt rural environment.

1. Stare at a patch of wild flowers which have their faces open to the sunshine, and while you are staring, try to imagine you are disappearing into the flowers, becoming part of them.

2. Find a rain drop which is sparkling in the sunlight. Squint your eyes and you will see a tiny blaze of rainbow colours. Imagine you are disappearing through the centre of that blaze.

3. Sit quietly in the woods or garden.With your eyes closed, imagine you can still see the scene around you and look into it carefully.This needs ten minutes with your eyes closed. Be prepared for a few surprises!

4. Let go of any anger or resentment you are carrying. Fairies are highly sensitive and will only approach if you are calm and loving.

Look only for good.

When you meditate, or try to see fairies, look only for good, and you will see only good. All things which express joy and love and are working harmoniously to enhance the beauty of this earth are of God.

'We have come to fish for the herring fish

That live in this beautiful sea,

Nets of silver and gold have we'

Said Wynken, Blynken and Nod.

Eugene Field

Chapter 3
The Gold Web

Fairies and Ley Lines

Fairy Pathways

Fairy Rings

Chapter 3
The Golden Web

Fairies And Ley Lines

Under the lilac tree in our Somerset garden was a boat-shaped hollow. On a sunlit morning, at the age of five, I was playing there with a friend, Paul, when the light suddenly changed. A golden web had come down, enclosing me in a shimmering dome. Paul was outside, still playing, apparently unaware of the change.

Triangles of light flickered through the dome, the colour blue blended with the sound of singing. Scented lilac blossoms nodded in the sky, and fairies were sitting in the branches.They were forget-me-not blue and motionless, arms and wings folded, skirts curved out like blue umbrellas.Faces so small, so misty and soft, emanated benevolence from dreaming sapphire eyes.The hems of their clothes were raspberry and saffron, accentuating the blue. Sound and colour seemed inextricably linked in an endless heavenly choir, singing against the backcloth of fragrance and sun bright leaves and sky.

Contented stillness distinguished these forget-me-not fairies from their more active contemporaries. They were just being, not doing, being. Some great event seemed imminent, for they were all gazing down into the hollow where I sat in a red hand-knitted cardigan, a flowery dress and brown Clarks sandals. The fairies were waiting for something to happen to this ordinary lumpish child.

I looked down into the hollow with suddenly Xray eyes, through the leaf mould and tufts of new grass, past the worms and into the rock. Deep in the earth was a golden beam, a laser of pure light. It pointed to the Church, a St. Michael and All Angels. My eyes followed the golden beam far across the earth, and along its path were churches, stone circles and celtic crosses. In that moment I could see for a hundred miles to a cloud capped island where the golden beam left the land and curved on to a blazing Atlantic horizon. A ley line!

It was the 1940's. No one talked about ley lines then. Yet the fairies had shown me one. They were forget-me-not fairies, the name of the flower intended to seal the memory forever.

'Mum I saw a golden line in the earth.'

'Oh yes dear.'

'The fairies showed it to me.'

'Did they dear?'

'And I was under a net of bright light.'

'Get your hands washed and don't talk nonsense.'

Ley lines were rediscovered in the 1920's by Alfred Watkins. High on a hill in Herefordshire, Watkins had a vision of a golden network of lines stretching far across the country, linking ancient sites and holy places. Churches, menhirs, mounds, ponds, holy wells, beacons, crosses etc. Excited by this vision Watkins spent a lifetime researching and proving its truth.

His book 'The Old Straight Track' has become a classic work for scholars of sacred geometry, or geomancy.

Watkins initially thought that ley lines were ancient way-marked trading tracks for such prehistoric necessities as flint, salt or clay. But later in his life he became convinced that ley lines had a deeper meaning, an energy and power, particularly where two ley lines intersected. Dowsers found that ley lines are part of a natural terrestrial energy flow, like the nervous system of the earth. All ancient sites, including Christian churches were sited by divination, or dowsing, placing them upon the power of ley lines to give maximum spiritual awareness to those who used them.

Ley lines are usually straight alignments of prehistoric sites which can be plotted on Ordnance Survey Maps - but there are wandering terrestrial energy flows such as the dragon current, the Lung-Mei, used and understood for centuries in China.

Ley-line places attract fairies and nature spirits.They live where the energy is at its maximum. The mathematics of an octahedral fairy city suggests that fairies construct their own ley-lines, for their palaces have a complex inner structure, a golden web.' Interesting that the colour gold always predominates. Alfred Watkins described his vision as a network of golden lines, my own vision was of a golden beam, and the fairies themselves have told me they weave webs of gold.

The golden web is a mysterious thing. If you see it, you will never forget it. On the night my mother died, I watched her soul pass over. She travelled at incredible speed, over a rainbow shaped archway, and at the sixty degrees point her face passed into a web of burning gold, criss-crossing lines that fizzed and sparkled like fireworks. Gradually her image dissolved into this complex shining network, and I knew she had finally gone. A psychic friend later confirmed to me that many souls go through a golden web when they die, perhaps we all do.

Fairy Pathways

Fairies create their own pathways just as foxes and badgers do, and these are laced with etheric silver and gold. Spiders often choose fairy paths to spin gossamer threads, adding rainbows to the energy. If left alone, a fairy path will grow its own canopy of ferns and the stones will be carpetted with mosses. Trickling rainwater contributes jewels and refreshment to these secret paths which can still be found in wild places. How painful to contemplate the effect of the plough and the building of motorways, obliterating these beautiful fairy ways.

On the sea cliffs it is easy to see fairy paths meandering through the clumps of wild flowers. The grass along these paths is of a brighter green and often glazed with wet gossamer. Fairy paths are cool places, even in the noon day sun, and if you were small enough to walk in one, you would see sea pinks arched overhead like cherry trees, and white campion like parasols.

The sunken roads of the elves are much larger than fairy paths. Designed to accommodate beings of four to five feet in height, these are narrow roads going between high stone banks, often overhung with trees creating a green twilight. Elf roads stretch for long distances, even hundreds of miles across country. Many have been widened into roads, but remnants of them can still be found.

Elf roads were linked by ponds, wells and streams. Pools were constructed in long alignments to mirror the rays of the sun at certain times of the year, forming a necklace of reflected light which could be followed. Although most of the pools have disappeared, these lines can be traced on old maps.

Processions of fairies and elves still travel along its old roads and paths, and over etheric bridges in the sky. In the summer of 1997 I was lucky to witness the coming and going over such a bridge at St. Michael's Mount in Cornwall.

On a glittering day in August, I sat with my back against the stone pillar outside the castle on top of the mount. With determined effort I soon became oblivious to the crowds of visitors milling around me. In the heart meditation you 'hear the small bird singing and not the traffic.'

A vision of a golden archway came to me. Rainbow-like it stretched a high bridge over the sea to the headland beyond. It was like a celestial motorway with multi-coloured beings coming and going, all of them in pastel robes which swirled and billowed as they drifted. Some had crystal wings, and others just sailed effortlessly. The dominant colour was gold, like those golden evenings of late summer. The feeling was of love and music, and a sense of the ethereal world parallel to ours.

Fairy Rings

Fairy rings in folklore have been linked to the bright green mushroom rings, and this may be so, but there are greater rings, and golden ones. Sacred places on earth are often encircled by a fairy ring which has been there for centuries.The ring is energising and beneficial to plant and mineral life, and particularly to water. Providing the ring remains unspoilt, then we too can benefit from its energy.

The circle is a symbol of eternity, and thousands of years ago mankind built stone circles and camps inside existing fairy rings. Some of these rings were miles in diameter, and inevitably they have been damaged by the building of towns and roads.Working with a group of dedicated earth healers, I witnessed the healing of one of these fairy rings.

I had always sensed a force field around Glastonbury, about sixteen miles across and corresponding to the outer limits of the landscape zodiac.There was one particularly bad place, an accident black spot, on a busy road, the old pilgrim way between Bridgwater and Glastonbury, and it was here that we did our work on a cold November day.

'Our Work' involved being willing to be used, to give our love and energy to healing this place, and to trust that we were protected by the archangel Michael. Flexible prayer is allowing your whole self and soul to be an instrument for the tune that is needed for healing.

'But what do you actually DO?' My puzzled neighbour asked me. 'Just stand there with your eyes shut?'

'Well - yes. It isn't physical work. It's the work of the soul. When you pray you just stand there with your eyes shut don't you?'

'Yes but I'm praying.'

'So are we.'

'But what prayers are you saying?'

'We aren't saying words. We're allowing the light to flow through us. It's like healing. You just stand there and ask the Holy Spirit to flow through you.'

'But why heal a fairy ring?'

'Because its been wounded by the activities of humans.'

On that misty day, 'just standing there with our eyes shut' allowed us to see how damaged the fairy ring had become. It was marbled with millions of faces, souls ensnared in wartime battles, and within it lurked the darker darkness of a planet in crisis.The ring was not still, but speeding like the rings of Saturn around the planet of Glastonbury which shone like a glass ball, its lower hemisphere deep in the earth.

We visualized ourselves growing, filled with the radiance of the spirit, and in that moment we did indeed grow as souls. We became huge beings of light, miles tall, stretching out our blazing swords to touch its centre. Like a floodlit wheel we began to spin at tremendous speed until we matched the speed of the ring, transforming it brighter and brighter as we passed.

Slowly a rose pink healing glow covered us and clearly the ring was changing. Celestial fire burned fiercely along its edges, and each white flame gradually changed into one petal of a sixteen mile lotus.The four of us disappeared completely for a few seconds, absorbed totally by the light and speed of this healing.

In those precious seconds of being invisible, I saw the fairies in their thousands. Flocks of them streamed down the hills towards the ring, trailing tassels of gold. Multi-coloured sparks raced beside them, entering the ring. They came from North, South, East and West, swarming over tree-tops and roof tops, and rising up from the river valleys in clouds of celebration.

Colours washed in and out of the ring, purple, then deep blue, emerald, marigold and pink and finally white. Watching the white come in,I knew our work was done and the darkness of the ring was gone forever. It was luminous gold, a true fairy ring full of energy and love, and the fairies were there to welcome its restoration.

'Look at the stars! look, look up at the skies
O look at all the fire-folk sitting in the air!
The bright boroughs, the circle-citadels there!
Down in the dim woods the diamond delves!
  the elves eyes!'

Gerard Manley Hopkins

Chapter 4

Where The Fairies Live

Diamond Cities

Lord of the Green Earth

Is it your Imagination?

A Fairy Guide to a Public Garden

Chapter 4

Where The Fairies Live

Diamond Cities

The fairies live in diamond shaped cities. These are invisible to us. They are etheric, that is made of a material which vibrates at a different frequency, so we cannot see it with our physical eyes. We may be able to enter a fairy city at their invitation in a meditative state. Certainly a body cannot enter - but a soul can.

The cities are octahedral, like two pyramids joined at the base having eight triangular facets, six points and eight edges. The size is unmeasurable since it can change at will, being exquisitely small in some situations and vast in others. Colours are spectrum colours, those of pure light rainbows.

The fairy cities hang in the air in ancient woodland, in sacred gardens and rocky gorges, close to watering places, and where there is an abundance of wild plants, mosses and fungi. Old apple trees and elderberry trees are popular, and sheltered pockets of sea cliffs. Sometimes the whole city is within the rock, or within an old tree or a green hillside.

Fairy cities are not static. They can move to another place. The whole city moves as a unit.

Back in the seventies, when the elm trees were dying of Dutch Elm disease, and the book ' Silent Spring ' was on everyone's lips, I had the rare privilege of unexpectedly entering a fairy city.

I was sitting under beech trees one summer afternoon, and idly gazing at a golden spark of sunlight on a raindrop, squinting my eyes to see the rainbows in it. The spectrum blazed pinks and greens, and stained-glass blue. Closer squinting produced a tiny blaze from each point of light. The intense concentration caused a state of mind similar to meditation in which you suddenly find yourself in another world.

A figure was sitting eerily beside me on the moss. For some reason it seemed unwise to look directly at him, but there was an awareness of light flickering over his green skin.

'Welcome' he spoke in a voice somewhere between a bee and a breeze 'You have entered our kingdom.'

'How did I get here?'

'You came in through the point of infinity.'

'Through the centre of the spark on the raindrop?'

'That's right.Few can enter our world for it is long forgotten. But you have special gifts.'

While he was talking I stared around me in wonder. Everything glittered so brilliantly it was difficult to see what was there. I concentrated on patches of phosphor-essence and they were filled with figures, little rainbow folk with soft berry faces and clothes of gossamer. They were not like any pictures of fairies that have ever been drawn for they oscillated and changed constantly like reflections in water. Behind them stood taller figures, rank upon rank of them in paler colours. The oddest thing was that the perspective seemed to be reversed. Instead of getting smaller and fainter in the distance, these beings grew larger and more brilliant until the distance was such a shimmering radiance that I had to look away.

Lord Of The Green Earth

'The face of mankind is turned towards the destruction of this planet.'

The voice of the tall green figure beside me became compelling, forcing me to turn and look fully into his green moss eyes. Love and fear and hostility looked back, stirred by the intensity of having only a moment to channel an immense task.

'What do you mean?'

'It is inevitable,' he folded his green hands and his knuckles interlocked like tree roots. 'All humans are doing it. Making machines. Creating chemicals that kill birds and insects and plants, and alienating the fairy kingdoms. Look, I'll show you.'

He showed me a mighty beam of light, a searchlight that seemed to shine across the world. Millions of wild creatures were trapped in it, vast swarms of every kind of insect, flocks and flocks of birds lay dead. Trees were in there too, my beloved elm trees, dead like white bones picked clean in the coppery sun. Then he showed me space with the stars bedimmed and the earth floating and twisting, dead like the moon. And then the beam of light curved and turned back and the green earth began to live again crowds of humans lined the path, sitting in total stillness, their palms upturned to the sky. Flowers grew around them like rainbow stars.

'Know me!' said Pan 'I am Lord of the Green earth.'

While he spoke a transformation took place, like something out of Star Trek. Points of light shone out from inside his skin until the whole being was a network of stars. Diminishing diamonds of green soon became absorbed by the white light, and only his pale aura lingered beneath the trees, emanating peace. The air tasted of autumn, but was heavy with the tang of sap. The lime tree sang with bees, and flute like echoes still came from the fairy city as if somehow it was moving away from me like a balloon.

Is It Your Imagination?

That experience of meeting Pan was remembered in a regression workshop years later. It helped me to see the earth through new eyes, and to understand that nature spirits are present in their thousands, beavering away to assist the growth of plants. They are in the wind and in the water, and within the earth itself.

When you are in a garden which is loved, you are surrounded by these energetic light beings. Ironically the best way to see them is to close your eyes. This cuts through the screen of physical seeing and allows your inner vision to operate.

'Is it my imagination?'

'Yes, and no.'

'How can that be?'

'Your imagination is a powerful instrument. Yes it creates things, but it can film what is really there.'

'But how can you tell the difference?'

'You discipline it by focussing. For example, ask it to show you what is in a particular tree. Wait, and it will show you.'

'But how can you prove it?'

'When a group of us see the same thing, as often happens. Working on your own is harder, but you must cultivate acceptance. Welcome what you see, and encourage your inner vision to become active again.'

'Active again?'

'When you were a child your inner vision worked perfectly. Its been damaged by years of conditioning from humans- not from God! Remember - become as a little child'

A group of us worked on our inner vision in this way, focussing, asking and cultivating acceptance. We chose a much loved public garden, and it was humbling to find that fairies are not just hiding in remote corners of Britain.They are everywhere, ignoring humans and getting on with their work industriously. Twelve of us spent just one hour of a summer morning in this garden, working in groups of three.

In silence we sat in different parts of the garden, closed our eyes and focussed on one area, asking to be shown what was really there. Then we compared our experiences, and in each group all three had seen the fairies. Together we compiled a 'fairy guide book' to the garden. Here it is.

A Fairy Guide To A Public Garden

As you enter this garden you will see colonies of shining green gnomes working inside the rocks. Pause to watch them energising the minerals within, so that every rock scintillates with light. Touch the rock and allow the crystal life to invigorate your aura.

Walk through the stone entrance pillars, and on the lawn directly in front of you is the landscape angel, twenty foot tall, and clothed in swirling radiance. From the mist, flotillas of coloured stars are leaving for different parts of the garden, or arriving back to be re-absorbed into the angel's light.

The garden is full of tourists on this hot summer day. Their auras illuminate the air, in lemon, and aquamarine and coral.

The first tree you come to is a crab apple in full blossom. Look inside the trunk. A fountain of shimmering light rises from the roots, shedding its bright rain into the curving branches. Over the blossoms hundreds of minute fairies are smothering the tree in sequins of light.

Now turn left into the pine walk. These pine trees are centuries old, and their light system is emerald and terracotta. Vertical rods of light play up and down the tall trunks. Higher up, the sprays of pine needles support thousands of singing fairies. Listen, and you will hear their high-pitched choirs, their twangling bells and the responsive whisper of the wind. Breathe in the scent of pine to sharpen your awareness. Stand with your back against the tallest pine, and observe the ley line which sweeps through the wood like a silver road. In the distance you can see it piercing the church and carving a tunnel of light through the mountains.

At the end of the pine walk is the lake. The luminous orbs floating in the water are clusters of water fairies resting. Don't miss the green and white dancing figures around the waterfall, these are vigorous water sprites enjoying its tumbling water. The phosphorescent coils under the surface which give its lake its own light are water plant fairies who can be seen shining on dark afternoons and, spectacularly, at night.

Beside the lake is the king oak tree, teeming with oak fairies and busy gnomes. This is a prayer oak. Take time to pause, be still, and breathe its breath. The oak light is bedimmed and restful. Each leaf is a green hand cupping twilight. Beneath the oak you will hear the hum of countless beings. Hum your own note, aloud, and hear the response grow into a resounding OM from this mighty tree and its inhabitants. Watch the ripples go out across the lawns.

In autumn take care not to step on the plump acorns which have fallen from the prayer oak. The fairies and gnomes gather them and take them flying along the ley lines to plant other prayer oaks far away. If you wish to take some, be sure that you will plant them and lovingly nurture them into trees.

Return through the flower garden, and take this opportunity to send your love to the thousands of fairies who work here through the seasons. They carry the life-force, enrich the colours and coax perfume from flowers. Deep in the stems these life sparks assist the programme of each flower, and imbue each seed with knowledge of how and when it must grow, when to live and when to die and how to be reborn.

'Ye elves of hills, brooks, standing lakes and groves
And ye that on the sands with printless foot
Do chase the ebbing Neptune, and do fly him
When he comes back.'

William Shakespeare - The Tempest

Chapter 5

The Piskies

The sacred springs -

A prediction comes true

Machine friendly piskies

Please talk to me!

Chapter 5

Piskies

The Sacred Springs - A Prediction Comes True

After the remembering, I learned to see the fairies regularly, and found them in all sorts of places.Inside roses and on the tops of teasels. Dancing on the lawns of Glastonbury Abbey, and in the cobbled walls of Lindisfarne. Twisting through cornfields, staring out from stones, speeding through wave tunnels in Cornwall. So elusive!

Seeing the fairies is not enough. You must use all your senses to build a whole experience. The sound of fairies is cleverly blended into other sounds, to hear it you can cultivate selective listening, disentangling their singing and laughter from an orchestra of birdsong, the wind in the trees, and the sound of rushing water. Fairy fragrance is very close to flowers, but subtly different, enticingly mysterious. And sometimes the presence of fairies will create a taste in the air, a hint of honey on the tongue, or bitter lemons. Rock gnomes leave a tang of minerals.

Touch is excluded. To touch a fairy must be the ultimate privilege. I have never touched one and can only imagine how they would feel. Fairies are not physical, and so perhaps this most basic of our senses does not count. But your sixth sense will be quite electric if you try to <u>sense</u> nature spirits around you! Their vibrations will cause your skin to tingle, your hair to prickle, and your breath to proceed with the utmost caution in case it should blow the fairy away.

It was mortifying to have this remote awareness of the fairies, fascinating but not satisfying. Judging by the wealth of fairy folklore, the fairies used to talk to us. Communicating with them did not happen until I came to live in Cornwall, and it was a privilege which had to be earned.

Our home, is on the Lizard Peninsula close to the Helford river, an unspoilt and sparsely populated area. Ancient oak woods hang over winding creeks, and there are vast tracts of heathered moorland uncultivated since the dawn of time. The coastline extends from the opal seas of Falmouth bay round to the rugged rocks and flower-rich cliffs of the Lizard, the most southerly point in Britain. Geologically it is one of the oldest pieces of land on earth.

A landscape zodiac aligned to the Star Deneb was laid out here three thousand years ago by an unknown civilization, perhaps Sumerians, Phoenicians, or even visitors from outer space. Our home is in the heart of the dove figure which is inside Leo the Lion.

The old Cornish name for our land means 'enclosure with springs.' It is sacred ground, surrounded by a golden fairy ring, and set in a sheltered hollow 100ft above the sea. The quality of silence here is so sharp that you can hear the burr of a sparrow's wings, the distant rhythm of the sea, and bell tones from over the bay.

Three ley lines cross in the old farm yard which is cloistered by apple orchards, vineyards, and woods. Here the Druids gathered, and Cistercian Monks prayed in the chapel barn. The massive stones of serpentine and granite have absorbed and stored their songs forever. Below the level of the farm yard, seven springs rise from the ancient woodland, like the seven sacred springs of the Kingdom of Logres.

How I ended up here is an extra-ordinary story. Ten years ago while meditating on Ivythorn Hill in the heart of the Somerset Leo figure, the following words were channelled to me.

<u>You will come to Cornwall, to live in a place called Hallowglen, and there in a corner by a hawthorn tree you will find a holy well with seven sacred springs, and the piskies will be there to help you.</u>

I searched maps, libraries and Cornish dictionaries for Hallowglen, and there was no such place. Spiritual matters were far from my mind when Ted invited me here, but when he showed me the woodland glen with its spring gushing from the hillside, and told me that the woods were full of springs which used to supply the whole village with water, it began to dawn on me that this was 'Hallowglen.' (The glen of Port<u>hallow</u>) The prediction was proved to be true. I did come to live here, as Ted's wife. Solomon, my black and white cat who is fifteen and good at seeing fairies, came with me to keep an eye on us!

But where were the other six of the sacred springs? The search for them has taken a year, and it began with my determined efforts to talk with the Cornish Piskies.

Machine Friendly Piskies

Have you ever bought one of those little brass piskies in a tourist shop in Cornwall? Surprisingly the real piskies are remarkably similar, golden in colour and about nine inches high. Like the fairies they blaze so brightly that it is difficult to distinguish features.

I first met real piskies in an unexpected way. You'd expect piskies to keep well clear of hefty farm machinery - not so the Cornish piskies. Lying in a corner was an ancient standing stone, covered in moss and guarded by rock gnomes who were very hostile. It took me three weeks to make friends with them and assure them of our intention to restore the stone to its original standing place on the ley line in the opposite corner of the field. Seeing these rock gnomes was not easy, for they lurked furtively within the stone, and only their watchful eyes were obvious.

The yellow digger we had hired came rumbling into the field and I explained to the driver how the stone was to be moved. At that moment a line of sparkling gold appeared along the top of the hedge. An army of Cornish piskies were advancing like Zulus! Their chattering sounded like hundreds of those bobbly bells that Morris Dancers sew on their socks. Then the roar of the digger's engine obliterated everything.

Why had the piskies come? Was it a war? Would they some how prevent us moving the stone? Anxiously we watched the driver manoeuvring the massive stone, the metal teeth biting into the soil beneath. What if he broke it? Gouging noises, a few shunts, and then, success. The stone was prised from its bed trailing festoons of grass and nettles, and lifted high into the air like an offering to the stars.

The reaction from the piskies was a riot of excitement. The golden line of light blazed into life, oscillating vigorously like a pulse on a screen. It was still not clear whether they were hostile. What if he dropped the stone or had a terrible accident?

Diggers have always seemed clumsy and aggressive to me, the most undesirable of machines to have around and guaranteed to banish all wild life including fairies. But here was a digger performing with such sensitivity and gentleness. Carrying the stone aloft, the digger paraded across the field. The piskies reaction was positive. There were celebrating!

Bouncing and bounding over the grass they swarmed after the digger, around it and over it. Even above the engine their laughter was ringing.

The stone was lowered into position, the digger respectfully retreated and the piskies closed ranks in a golden ring, and began to dance. With high knees and spiky hands, the dance continued for about twenty minutes, and then, at the stroke of noon, all the piskies melted into the grass like butter into toast.

Please Talk To Me!

The next time the piskies appeared it was by invitation! Walking through Porthallow woods every day, I sent out silent thoughts to the fairies. This is THOUGHT TELEPATHY. We can all do it. Most of us can send our thoughts but have not learned how to receive thoughts. Spirit people, and even animals, are more receptive to thought telepathy than we are. They can send it and receive it.

By thought telepathy I told the fairies about our plans for planting wild flowers and trees, and how we loved and accepted them as part of God's creation. They stayed out of sight, but they were in there listening and watching. On the day we started building a herb sundial, my patience was rewarded.

Before the first brick was laid, I went into the woods and told the fairies, by thought telepathy, what we were going to do, and explained that the herbs would bring perfume and bees and butterflies to them. I asked for their help and returned to the yard where Ted and Dave were mixing cement.

A line of sparkling gold emerged from the woods, along the ground. Watching it with intense concentration I saw to my joy that it was a procession of Cornish Piskies. They filed right into the yard and sat high up along fences and walls. They seemed excited, but stayed in lines as if fearful of stepping into the open in the presence of humans. After about an hour the piskies had gone, except for one who stayed crouched on a post until dark, a sort of look-out scout.

He left at sunset, and I followed his amber light along the woodland path. Surprisingly it kept pausing, as if he was leading me.

On the old tithe maps, one of our fields is called Well Field. The piskie led me to where this meadow sloped steeply into an overgrown boggy area, and there he sat on a curving sycamore branch. The other piskies were sitting along it with straight backs and folded limbs. Looking closely at their lights sparkling in the dusk, I noticed that each piskie carried a tiny lantern on a stick, but the source of the light was a mystery. This branch was the piskies favourite gathering place, directly above the sacred springs which we had yet to discover.

'I really need you to talk to me' I said aloud.

Silence.

Perhaps telepathy would work.

'Please talk to me.'

Silence. One by one the lanterns rose and disappeared into the twilight.

'I come from haunts of coot and hern

    I make a sudden sally,

  And sparkle out among the fern

    To bicker down a valley.'

        Alfred Lord Tennyson - The Brook

Chapter 6

Elbino

The blue fairy speaks

A promise in fairy language

The place of many waters

A bedraggled black object

Elbino and the cat

Chapter 6

Elbíno

The Blue Faíry Speaks

Elbino is definitely a cut above the other fairies. For one thing she is undoubtedly female, she is big, about two feet high, predominantly blue in colour and has visible wings. And she speaks English. No messing with telepathy. Elbino talks.

Joan and I were meditating in the conservatory one afternoon, not expecting anything in particular to happen. Joan is a spiritual person, but down to earth and wickedly humourous. She is sixty-something, and she has never retired, spending her incredible energy teaching reflexology to nurses and campaigning to enlighten the medical profession.If you asked Joan whether she believed in fairies, she would look at you as if you'd asked whether fire is hot.

'I've always known them' she'd say. 'The little darlings.'

If you show Joan a photograph of anything with trees, flowers and rocks in it, she immediately points out the fairies.

'Look at this little fellow! Hiding in the cherry tree,' or 'Look at those little darlings in the grass.'

Joan is full of love and joy. No wonder the fairies show themselves to her. But on this occasion something happened to Joan which had never occurred before, in her life or mine.

We sat in meditation, eyes closed, palms upwards, oblivious to external sounds. Distant tractors, helicopters, someone hammering down in the village, the whine of the washing machine, none of these sounds registered. But into our silence came an exquisite fairy voice.

'May I speak with you?'

The tiny voice had perfect diction.It sounded shy and polite, but persistent.

'May I speak with you?'

Three times it asked, until it dawned on me that a response was required!

'Please do. You are welcome.'

My voice is soft but it sounded thunderous in comparison. There was a pause. Had my giant voice blown it away? Then the tiny voice spoke again.

'At the time of the flowering of the apricot, you will come to the place of many waters.'

Silence.

'Who are you?' I asked.

'My name is Elbino.'

'Where is the place of many waters?'

'You will find it.'

No more information was given. We came out of our meditation. No one else was there. We both agreed Joan had channelled a fairy, yet the fairy had not appeared.

Trying to make sense of what Elbino had said, the memory of planting apricot stones last May came to mind. The stones had germinated and grown rapidly into trees, planted in response to channelled information. Centuries ago Apricot trees flourished here in groves from stones which St. Keverne had brought from Italy.

A Promise In Fairy Language

Elbino appeared at the well the following day. She came mistily at first, two gauzy wings folded down her back. She seemed born out of the blue air, gold rimmed and pale skinned. Her eyes were lamps in her thoughtful face which was wider at the brow and more pointed at the chin than a human face, a generous heart shape topped by a velvety pixie hat. Her skin had the silken quality of sea water. She stood with her legs wide apart, and her long fingers moved though the air as if she were playing a harp. She smelled of wet bluebells.

Something else set Elbino apart from other fairies. She was sad. I had never seen a sad fairy before. My concern reached cosmic proportions as we stared deeply into each other's eyes. Smiling was inappropriate. Elbino was depressed. Silently she beckoned me to follow her into the wood. She tiptoed, without using her wings, leading me along the path under a twilight of sycamores.

It was mediaeval woodland. The twigs were bearded with ashen and mustard coloured lichens. Every branch was a garden built from green pennywort, and hemispheres of moss and ferns rooted into the bark. Fallen trees had remained for centuries, and coppiced up again, supporting palaces of fungi. But underfoot it was black bog, in fact the mud was navy blue and stinking judging by the state of a friend's golden retriever who had ventured in there!

No one had walked there in living memory. Only the cattle sploshed through it, making winding paths of liquid mud. So why was Elbino leading me into this inaccessible place? It dawned on me that she was following the same path as the piskies had done, to their favourite branch.

Solomon the cat ran ahead of us, flicking his ears back to hear my following footsteps. When we reached the gate into Well field, he sat down, boldly confronting the herd of bullocks who stood with lowered heads inside the gate. I wasn't going to go in there with them even for Elbino!

The fairy disappeared to the left into a mass of bramble, bobbing her blue wings as she lurched her way through it. There was something suicidal about the way she was moving. Solomon sat to attention, obviously watching her. He and the bullocks and I all looked very serious.

'Promise!'

Elbino's tiny voice came to me like a bell ringing. With a burr of wings she stood before me again, and her expression was fierce, her shoulders square and her eyes tormented. Solomon went raging up the sycamore tree, and sat there miaowing on the piskie branch.

'Promise what Elbino?'

49

'Promise you will stop the cattle coming into the wood. They have destroyed the place of many waters.'

'How have they done that?'

'Once this was a beautiful meadow with clear springs and waterfalls. We loved to dance along the streams. Now look at it.' Elbino waved a desperate arm towards the wood. There were no streams visible or audible, only a tangle of brambles and pools of mud.

'Until the streams run clear again we cannot work with you.' she said. 'Promise.'

'We'll do our best.'

Elbino looked at me quizzically for a long time. She didn't believe me.

'How do you promise in fairy language?' I asked.

'You pick a green leaf and hold it against your heart.'

I duly repeated the promise with a fat sycamore leaf clapped to my chest, and Elbino smiled at last. The smile produced such radiance that suddenly she was gone into the light, and Solomon came down from the tree immediately. I wagged a finger at the bullocks.

'You lot have had it.'

The Place Of Many Waters

A husband who takes these matters seriously is a great blessing. Within the week a fence was erected and the cattle were banished from the wood forever. Restoring the

'Place of Many Waters' took us a year of snipping and shovelling. First we cleared an acre of bramble, revealing an ancient meadow with a meandering boggy patch. Through the winter we dug out the stream bed, delighted to find its bright pebbles and crystal water. We made new banks and planted cowslips and primroses. And in the spring, 'at the time of the flowering of the apricot,' we discovered, under the brambles, the source of this beautiful stream, a bubbling spring, not one but seven pure clear pools, the 'place of many waters.'

Elbino did not talk again for months, but she sometimes came and stood close to me like a cat. The feeling from her was vulnerability. She needed me. I kept on assuring her that work was in progress, the streams would be cleared as our limited time and physical strength allowed. But every day I was drawn to the 'place of many waters.' If anyone had asked my occupation at that time it would have been 'chief mud shoveller - especially in the rain.' A robin with a crippled foot kept me company, chattering like a ventriloquist with his beak shut and only his throat moving. He knew when Elbino came, for he would fly to her and sit adoringly at her feet, never moving until she had gone.

One day Elbino led me to the lower end of the wood, a secluded place, impossible to walk in because of bogs. For months she had been giving me accurate weather forecasts, and now she indicated a major blockage in the stream and asked me to clear it.

'Tomorrow there will be BIG RAIN.' Elbino said.

Clearing the blockage was tricky, but I managed it, and an absolute deluge followed. Twenty four hours of rain that scoured the landscape like a sweeping brush.

A Bedraggled Black Object

'What on earth is THAT?'

'Some kind of freak insect?'

A bedraggled black object was clinging to a cream chrysanthemum in cold sunshine. In the aftermath of prolonged rain, ribbons of water were curling down the path.

A closer look at the freak insect convinced me that it was an extremely wet bumble bee which had crawled up the flower in an attempt to dry itself out. Surprising what a thin little bee it looked with its fur plastered against its body, and its wings heavy like two paper clips.

Thinking motherly thoughts about thawing it out in the greenhouse and making it fluffy again, I went to fetch a jam jar. But Elbino intervened.

'Leave it alone' she said, only half appearing to me. Half her face, and one blue hand held up to stop me catching the bee. Well you don't argue with fairies!

Twenty four hours later, the bedraggled bumble was still clinging tenaciously to the cream chrysanthemum, and another bumble bee, in good condition, was sitting closely beside it. The two insects had their heads together, and the good bee had one front leg upon the bedraggled one, as if comforting it! Fascinated, I kept them under observation for about an hour, until a golden haze shone around them, the size of an egg. It shone only for a moment, and then the good bee rose and buzzed away.

Elbino was not there. So I furtively picked the whole flower with the sick bee attached and took it into the greenhouse. But the bee was already dead. Had Elbino brought the good bee to comfort his brother? Or do bumbles do this all the time?

Elbino And The Cat

Birds and animals do respond to the presence of fairies. Perhaps they are closer to them than we are. Unrestricted by the complexity of words, creatures communicate by telepathy. It is their first language. With us, telepathy has become our second language, mostly unused. Creatures have freedom from conditioning. You can teach a dog to sit, but you cannot train it not to see fairies!

Solomon, our cat, definitely knows the fairies, but he is picky about which ones he wants to associate with. His habit of tearing up a tree when Elbino appears looks like straight jealousy. But cats are energy sensitive and often choose to go up a few layers to where they can sit in peace, without having their fur charged up. If your cat wants to sit on top of the bookshelves, you can be sure there is too much energy in the room.

Siamese cats are particularly sensitive. Our weekly meditation group was in the home of two siamese cats who always headed for the top shelf as the room filled up with people. Once the meditation started, they would creep down and drape themselves purring over laps and feet.

Solomon stands back from the piskies, like you would from a football team. But I have seen him on the grass surrounded by a shining ring of fairies, his golden eyes bemused, like a professor visiting a toddler group.

'The kiss of the sun for pardon

The song of the birds for mirth

You are nearer God's heart in the garden

Than anywhere else on earth.'

Dorothy Gurney

Chapter 7
Flower Fairies

Clarissa Clover

Devas

The marigold deva

The lavender deva

The thyme deva

Salvia Bethelli

The sage deva

Matilda

The Dove and the Buttercup

Chapter 7
Flower Fairies

Clarissa Clover

'Why can't I find one?'

'Find what?'

'A four leaved clover. I always find them!'

'It's simple. You have to ask.'

Lara and I were walking across a meadow thick with clover, buttercups and grasses. Four leaved clovers had often appeared for me, usually on ley lines and sacred sites, but today they eluded me.

'You have to ask the clover fairy.' Lara said 'You say - Clarissa Clover find me a four leaved clover please.'

Swiftly she bent down and picked a perfect four leaved clover, and gave it to me.

'How come I didn't see it! Such a big one.'

'It wasn't there when you looked. Clarissa Clover manifests them.'

Lara knew more about fairies than I did at the time. A fairy had lived among her pot plants in her Chelsea flat for years, and had moved house with her to Somerset.

Since that amazing demonstration Clarissa Clover has often helped me to find four leaved clovers for people. I walk past our clover patch daily, and never see one. But if a visitor comes, a four leaved clover is always there on request, standing up prominently saying 'pick me.' Once I wanted three, one each for the friends who were with me. We stopped by the clover patch and there were three four leaved clovers, one right at the feet of each person. Even two bemused Ministry of Agriculture men left with four leaved clovers clutched wonderingly between finger and thumb.

Devas

The flower fairy books were an enriching part of my childhood. From them I learned to identify all the wild flowers, and to know whether they were medicinal or poisonous, or liked by bees. But I have never actually seen a flower fairy like the ones in the pictures.

But Devas definitely exist. The word Deva, in Sanskrit, means 'Shining one,' and it is used to describe the spirit of a particular plant, for example a bluebell deva is the essence of all bluebells. Devas do not always appear, but they do communicate and are happy to channel information about the plant. To listen to a Deva, you need to sit close to the plant you have chosen, and ask, telepathically, for it to talk to you. It will channel with surprising fluency and detail, be ready to write it down. Accept what it says. Acceptance is the key to receiving words. Intervene and the message will be lost.

Here are some channellings received from plant devas, faithfully recorded word for word, and not edited to suit this book!

The Marigold Deva

March 22nd AT 3.00 - After planting calendula.

I am aligned with your solar energy centre, the epicentre of your being. Warmth and radiance are within me. My structure is a reflection of solar fire, I am a dome, a hemisphere, my seeds are abundant and spiral. My perfume is deep and rich and should be inhaled by those of you who are weak and suffer tension in your solar plexus. Meditate upon my colour - the colour orange, there is no colour more warming and welcoming to the human eye. The fairies warm their hands upon my flowers. Their sensitivity is greater than yours, they can feel heat and cold and subtler emotional qualities from colours. Meditate on my true name - Marigold - Mary's Gold - the healing power and Godliness of simplicity, a simple cottage flower, now seldom grown but full of treasure. Thank you for planting me. I need more lime and lots of love.

The Lavender Deva

April 10th - After planting lavender at 4.00 on the herb sundial

The colour amethyst, the hue of the seventh ray comes out of the mist. It is a blend of red and blue, a perfect union, a fusion into LOVE from the red glow of the heart with the indigo ray of knowledge. The perfume of lavender penetrates deeply into the pituitary - take care, it is potent - stand back and breathe it from a distance, especially if you have dried the flowers.'

58

The Thyme Deva

April 23rd

Extreme complexity is my nature. I am like a geodetic dome, a crystalline structure. If you were the size of an ant you could sit beneath my domes and look up through a sunlit network of sticks and leaves into a universe of pink stars. The colour pink is the colour of music. Leave me alone and let me sing. Do not pick bits off me for you will destroy the delicate domes. You may take from the straggly thyme in the other herb garden by the wall!

Salvia Bethelli

(This wonderful plant is a hybrid between buddleia and sage.)

Respect the beauty of this new plant, Salvia Bethelli which is only here on earth because of the skill and understanding of mankind. This plant was created in a laboratory, and the breath of God was there at its moment of dawning. God breathed into it the most holy of colours, white and purple, and the most delicate luxurious structure of velvet. It was given the vigour of the buddleia and the potency of the sage. Respect it! This a hybrid - a joint creation between humankind and God - is this not cause for celebration? Treat this new plant with reverence. If you propagate it, explain why you are breaking bits off it, and give thanks to the life-force, the God breath within it.

The Sage Deva

Strength and power is my gift. I purify. Use me freely. Bunches of sage leaves hung in dark unpleasant places will clear bad energies. Breathe the aroma of sage deeply into your being, take in its strength, make tea from the leaves. Propagate me. Sage works in your emotional and chemical balance, clears your lymph system and brings positive attitudes. Keep a plant of sage close to you, even in winter, I will grow in a sunny window, especially the purple sage.

Allow me to flower each year, the bees adore the nectar. The cruellest thing a human can do to a plant is to prevent it from flowering, and this is like clipping the wings of a bird. To us plants, flowering is like flying, it is our high peak of fulfillment. Call it job satisfaction!

Matílða

Two hundred years ago a herbalist and healer, Matilda, lived in the now ruined cottage opposite our farmyard. Matilda has appeared to me several times. She is a homely figure with beaming blue eyes, wearing a green shawl and a long brown skirt and always with a pet wren on her shoulder.

'I hear you've seen a ghost.' A local person commented and I was shocked to hear Matilda described as a GHOST. Matilda is a soul who is happily settled in the spirit world. She occasionally chooses to talk to me in a helpful and interesting way sharing her unique knowledge of the history of this place, the fairy kingdom and the world of plants. She explained where to find the four- leaved clovers, and told me that apricots were grown here, and advised about the planting of wild flowers and herbs to benefit the birds, bees and butterflies.

Matilda is something of a missionary. She wants to spread good news and raise awareness of unseen wonders, of love and courage and good in the invisible realms. Matilda described a mystic experience which she had during her life in the cottage.

THE DOVE AND THE BUTTERCUP - BY MATILDA

The fairies weave webs around my cottage door, webs of silver and gold. At these times I hear words, and the fairies sit all around me and listen like children in school.

In the spring of 1807, a dove came to the glade, a pure white dove who sat upon the grass and walked about in the clover. Entranced by the shining white bird I sat outside my cottage without moving for I have never seen a pure white dove before.

As I watched a circle of light formed around the bird like a halo. The bird melted into this light which became burning bright, fizzling and sparking.

Then sound came from it, a rushing sound that suddenly changed into a whisper and I realised words were being spoken into the light. I listened intently and this is what I heard:

The golden ray is which you may use forever is brought to this place today by the holy dove it has travelled far through the heaven world from the star vega, passing through the holy hands of God like water being filtered.

The golden ray is focussed upon the earth and it shall be forever multiplied and reflected by a simple flower, a buttercup, and from this day the buttercup shall shine all over the earth and particularly in sacred places shall they cluster thickly.

The creative energising power of the colour yellow shall turn the darkness of man towards the face of God.

The long ages of dark are over.

Look forward into the light and store these words for generations to come.

You, Matilda, have a crystal clear aura through which we speak, and many after you will have these auras. Store these words in the memory banks of this glade which are invisible but have a structure of cells in an octagonal fashion.

After I heard these words the circle of light melted away softly as if it had never been.The dove remained and upon her breast was a shining yellow light, reflected from the buttercups. When the dove flew away, I looked where she had been and noticed for the first time in my life that the buttercups were indeed 'all over the earth' stretching to the far horizon, to the sea, and growing thickly to the edge of the woods.

I wrote the words down on a piece of wood and it took me three days. I did not have a pen or paper like yours. How I would have valued them! So I am happy to share these stories with you, otherwise they would remain forever hidden.

May God Bless you my dear.

Matilda

A story so beautiful you could even read it to your children. It reminded me of Moses and the burning bush when God's voice came out of the blazing light.

The fairies do like to sit with us and share spiritual experiences. At these times humans and fairies are very close under the umbrella of celestial love.

'Then came a flash brighter than all the rest,
and by the light of it - in the thousandth part of a
second they were gone again - but he had seen
them, he was certain of it - three beautiful
little white girls, with their arms twined round
each other's necks floating down the torrent, as
they sang, 'Down to the sea, down to the sea!'

Charles Kingsley - The Water Babies

Chapter 8

Water Fairies

A bridge of sparkles

A fairy in the greenhouse

Stop the video!

Chapter 8

Water Fairies

A Bridge Of Sparkles

Not by chance that fairies are sometimes described as ELEMENTALS (note the EL prefix again!) The four elements - earth, air, fire and water are homes for different types of fairies which are not so easy to see.

Attunement to the particular element is the best way of deliberately seeing them. With the exception of water fairies, you would be lucky to see these elementals although you may sense them.

Because our bodies are 70% water, we are already naturally attuned to the water element. Water is a major part of our relaxation, our cleansing, our recreation. Thousands head for the nearest lake or beach for leisure time, or seek out waterfalls, or swim. In the Age of Aquarius, water gardens are, becoming increasingly popular.

What do we want water to do? We want it to be still, to shine and reflect the sky. We want it to trickle and bubble and sparkle. We want it to roar over rocks making white rapids, and curl into crystal pools. Water fulfills the needs of all our senses.

If you sit close to water and meditate you are likely to see the water fairies, or hear them, or even feel them. Remember to send out loving thoughts, for the fairies will avoid someone who is angry or resentful. If you are feeling sad, or if your mind is in a turmoil, you can attune to the fairy kingdom by building a gratitude bridge out of sparkles. Here's how.

Begin by looking at the palms of your hands, and considering their beauty, their potential for kindness. Feel the sensitivity in the tips of your fingers, and marvel at the wonder of your hands. Say thank you for them, and visualize that thought as a tiny star of gratitude. Then choose another part of yourself, perhaps your eyes or ears, and create another star of gratitude. Look around you, and find reasons to be grateful. Nothing is too trivial. Sunshine, colours, air to breathe, a place to rest. All these things are great gifts to us.

The more you do this, the faster the bridge will grow. Visualize the sparkles merging into a glistening bridge. It is strong. Walk over it, and enter the place of joy and peace, you have a right to be there.

It is ideal to do this process close to water, for water sparkles and shines so abundantly. When you are in this beautiful frame of mind, you yourself become a shining being and the fairies will want to come close to you.

A Fairy In The Greenhouse

I first saw a water fairy from inside the greenhouse on a wet day. Rain was streaming down the glass, and brown bubbles were motoring past the door. The air was filled with diamonds, and looking deep into the silverness, I noticed delicate glassy beings weaving through the falling raindrops. As if through a zoom lens, I focused on one of them, the raindrops became huge pear drops, and there was one water fairy twisting and dancing among them. Fairies know if you can see them and they can disappear instantly, so I conveyed a friendly thought, by telepathy to this cellophane being. It fluttered to the greenhouse, and we regarded each other through the glass. In that moment I became small and the fairy large, so that we were equal, and neither felt threatened by the other. A good arrangement!

The fairy's skin shimmered, and tendrils of silver hair looped around her slim body. A robe of misted silk drifted over her shoulders to her feet, the edges of the fabric - if it was fabric - were hemmed with beads of water, and amethyst ribbons streamed from her waist. Her tiny hands were perfect, long, transparent with raindrop nails and a star on the tip of each finger.

But all this floating and twisting movement became a startled stillness as she clung to the greenhouse, looking in at me with frozen eyes.

'I send you love.' I said, by telepathy.

The eyes stayed frozen. They were amethyst.

'The rain is lovely.'

The fairy face rippled into a smile, and suddenly she was in the greenhouse. How she came in was not clear, but she probably came through the glass. She moved around, visiting each plant in turn, and appeared to be checking whether it was healthy. She took no notice of me, but the feel of her gliding to and fro was like being brushed with velvet. You'd expect a water fairy to be cold, but this one wasn't. Warmth trailed around her, and each time she passed close to my face it was like a breath on my skin, friendly and effervescent.

She spent a long minute loving a particular fern, her silver arms wrapped around it. Light shone from inside the fern, in that moment it was illuminated from within. Spirals of light came curling up from the soil, and the impoverished little fern grew into a splendid plant of pure light, a vision of how it could be. The fairy did not speak, but the message was clear. The fern must be put outside. A sheltered place by the stream came to mind.

Next she moved to the watering can, and gazed into it for a long time, her head on one side, and it seemed she wanted me to pick it up. When I did, there was a baby toad inside. Carefully I released it outside the greenhouse, and watched it crawl rapidly under a stone.

I returned to the greenhouse, and briefly saw a silver flash as the fairy departed, through the glass.

I planted the fern outside and it did grow into a flourishing energetic plant.

Stop The Video

Soon after this encounter, the water fairies began to help us restore our water garden.The first stream we had cleared was now burbling through an acre of meadow, rich with water parsnip and buttercup. The water fairies requested waterfalls, and they wanted the stream tuned to an octave! Tiny waterfalls at the source, tinkling bell sounds, wider ones, flatter ones, miniature gorges, some that splashed onto stones, others that poured into pools. And each waterfall had its own voice, growing deeper as the stream plunged towards the woods.

The octave, the water fairies told me, was the perfect eight, the octahedron, the shape of the fairy cities.

In Hebrew numerology, eight is the number of perfection. The octagon, in sacred architecture, represents order and harmony, a link of the circle, eternity, with the square, stability.

Water fairies can be seen in most watery places, and always in rainstorms. They are fast movers, whirling through the air so swiftly that you are unlikely to see them, unless you ask to 'stop the video.' Anything in spirit is possible! You can ask for movement to be halted so that you can look for a moment. It doesn't happen physically! The rain doesn't stop in mid air! The change is in you. Your perception is momentarily altered, and the results are quite spectacular, like looking into one of those 'magic eye' pictures.

Sometimes water fairies are still, usually early in the morning on a tranquil lake, so still that they are unrecognizable. They have changed from swirling dancers to mysterious shining blobs resting on the water surface, or coiled into emerald pools.

'The first foundation stone was jasper, the second sapphire, the third agate, the fourth emerald, the fifth onyx, the sixth carnelian, the seventh yellow quartz, the eighth beryl, the ninth topaz, the tenth chalcedony, the eleventh turquoise, the twelfth amethyst.'

Revelations 21-9 - The Bible

Chapter 9

Mineral Fairies

The being of the stone

Virgin of the rocks

A Pot-holer's experience of rock

Gnomes

How to see mineral fairies in Stones

Chapter 9

Mineral Fairies

The Being of the Stone

'You'd better have this.'

'What is it?'

'A lump of alabaster.'

I accepted the ungainly parcel, heaved it onto the train and took it home to Cornwall. Alabaster is a pink and white stone, similar to marble but softer. My father had often taken me to a nearby alabaster quarry to find lumps of it to carve into owls, frogs and dolphins. He used to run it under water as he sanded it, and the rosy pinks of it would glow translucent in the sunshine.

So despite the inconvenience of its weight, I felt nostalgic about lugging home this rose pink lump of Somerset, and dumping it unceremoniously in our Cornish kitchen. Undecided about where to put it, I left it there for three days, until a tiny voice called out as I walked past it.

'Oy!'

The voice was coming from the alabaster stone, and on top of it was an imperious white being, about nine inches tall. It was male, slender and elfin, but peppermint white all over, and the light that blazed out from it was whiter than light could ever be.There was an impression of a face, a wizardly triangle with pinhead eyes and an explosion of thistledown whiskers. His presence had great audacity and authority.If he'd been human, he would have been conducting an orchestra.

'Why have I been left here?' he asked, and without waiting for an answer, he continued, 'I am the being of this stone. I came out of the stone and it is a great effort for me to do that. See how tensely I must hold myself in order to talk to you. Are you going to keep still and listen to me?'

'Yes.'

'You humans are never still.You're worse than fairies. You're always dragging stuff here there and everywhere.'

'I promise to keep still.'

The pure white being stood stiffly, even his light seemed to stop blazing and freeze as he struggled to speak. I felt alarmed for him. He looked so old, and I wasn't sure whether fairies died, and what to do if he did!

'What I have endured to come here,' he said with a sigh and released some of his tension in little zig-zags of light while I watched, not daring to move. Obviously he had something important to tell.

'The stone must stay in the heart of the house. It is a gift, from the heart to the heart. Look at your maps and you will understand why.' The voice faded to a whisper and the little white being vanished into the alabaster.

What an assertive little man! Transfixed, I stared at the alabaster stone for about five minutes, not daring to touch it, but nothing happened. His disappearance was complete. Not a trace of light, not an echo of his voice remained, but there was a taste of burning magnesium in the air.

Gingerly I picked the stone up and carried it respectfully into the lounge, and placed it after much thought on its own small table, with a plant for company. The table lamp however was not welcome. Distinct vibes came out of the stone and I could almost hear the fierce little voice saying

'I don't want that electric stuff.'

The stone remains quietly in our lounge, and there have been no further visits from its charismatic inhabitant!

Curiously I studied the maps of Somerset and Cornwall. Around Glastonbury is a rare landscape zodiac, a set of huge figures drawn in the land by an ancient civilization. I was born inside the Leo the lion figure. When I came to Cornwall, I discovered a landscape zodiac here on the Lizard Peninsula, and found that our home is inside the lion figure. Coincidence?

I looked for the alabaster quarry, and was startled to see it right at the heart of the Somerset Lion. Now here was a piece of it, in the heart of the Cornish Lion. A fairy gift. From the heart to the heart.

Virgin Of The Rocks

A picture by Leonardo-Da Vinci, entitled Virgin of the Rocks is a compelling gaze.

It shows the Madonna and child Jesus reposing in a rocky cave. In the distance is a fairy tale landscape of sunlit hills and tiny towns under a sky graded from silver to sapphire. Marvellous rocks in rich browns have been painted in detail, showing every crevice and crack. And if you de-focus your eyes and look, as you would look at a 'magic-eye' picture, the secrets of the grotto reveal themselves. I believe that Leonardo's rocks not only contained rock-gnomes, but that the painter knew about them. It is this extra dimension which gives the picture its power and fascination - something beyond the paint which draws us deeper into our own sub-conscious, searching for truths we once knew. In past lives we lived alongside fairies and nature spirits. They were neighbours, as normal as birds and animals.

Memory is vast and limitless. Everything that ever happened to us, in this life and in previous lives, is there and can be accessed in regression therapy. I have re-lived four of my past lives in vivid detail, accurately describing places and incidents which I could not possibly have known about in this life. I have helped many other people through their regression, and heard them describe the fairies as if they were normal.

A retired nurse, Janet, told how she had been a cook in a previous life, in a huge Victorian kitchen. The fairies had always helped her to roll pastry and decorate pies. They had supervised the growing and drying of herbs in particular. And at night they had slept, Janet said, inside the walls - not in holes - but actually within the stone itself.

A Potholer's Experience Of Rock Gnomes

Experiencing rock fairies today can be more difficult because of tourism. Places like Cheddar Caves are full of rock spirits, but unless you have permission to enter the caves at a quiet time, your awareness will be muffled by the milling crowds. Pot-holers have golden opportunities to communicate, although they are often preoccupied with the mechanics of the sport. One hardened pot-holer described to me a time when he'd been alone in Wookey Hole cave, close to the underground river while waiting for his friends. He'd felt the rock gnomes presence strongly. Hordes of them. He'd seen their eyes looking at him solemnly from the walls. The experience sounds unnerving but Ian didn't find it so. He actually found it comforting, and shut his eyes to pray. Instantly the rock gnomes came close, he felt warmth from them, and friendliness. It was like a congregation, he felt the energy of their prayers. The prayers were communal worship, of the spirit of life, a celebration. The whole cave echoed with a sonorous humming, a sounding of the great 'om.'

How To See Mineral Fairies In Stones

Holding a smooth pebble is a good way of focussing your attention on its crystal energy. Crystals are part of God's creation. You accept crystals in your computer and quartz clock, you wear rings with diamonds or other precious stones. The earth is full of crystals. Crystals can be programmed by thought, and most people who use them program them with love, for healing and other positive gifts.

Choose a crystal, a single crystal, not a cluster. Hold it in your hand and pray for it to be cleansed of all negative influences. Run it under clear cold water, allow the sunlight to shine through it. Hold the crystal again and say 'I dedicate this crystal to the love and light of Christ.' Then give the crystal a specific purpose, it could be a forgiveness crystal or a friendship crystal, always something positive. Programming a crystal is similar to the church practice of lighting candles, putting a specific prayer into the candle flame, so you put a prayer into a crystal in the same way.

If you are patient and determined to visit a standing stone or rock when you can spend twenty minutes there in undisturbed silence, you will be rewarded. A highly sensitive person could feel the energy instantly, but most of us have to work at it. Concentrating on bringing the light into your heart, keeping very still with your eyes closed is essential.

Some like to meditate leaning against the stone. I prefer to sit down (otherwise I would fall over!) - close to the stone. Do whatever feels comfortable.

Focus on the stone and the space around it. Consider the earth below and the sky above. Do not do these things fleetingly. Take time to wait and allow pictures to come in. Fill in the detail of these pictures as if you were painting them.

Consider the distance beyond the stone in all directions. Perhaps memories of other places will come into your mind, places that may be linked with the stone, for all sacred sites are connected by a network of light paths.

The key word for you is WAIT. And the second is REMEMBER. When you go home, sit quietly and imagine yourself back there by the stone, write down what you felt. Its amazing what detail is stored in the memory, and unless we make an effort to remember, it will remain in storage!

Perhaps you will meet mineral fairies in this way. For me the ultimate experience which came from working by a standing stone was an encounter with the fairy medicine man who gave me a unique glimpse into fairy medicine and its links with homeopathy, crystals and music.

Sounds, and sweet airs,that give delight and hurt not
Sometimes a thousand twangling instruments
Will hum about mine ears; and sometimes voices
That, if then I had waked after a long sleep
Will make me sleep again.

William Shakespeare - The Tempest

Chapter 10

Secrets of the Fairy Medicine Man

The big buzz

The Medicine Man speaks

Fairy Medicine

Chapter 10

Secrets of the Fairy Medicine Man

The Big Buzz

The fairy medicine man appeared to me close to the granite stone where the piskies had been dancing.His arrival was unexpected.

Most fairies filter through the light into our vision, but the fairy medicine man came via sound and fragrance. It was three o'clock on a still afternoon in May, the time is significant for it is part of the 3, 6, 9, 12 vibration of numerology.These are the best hours to meditate, three o'clock, six o'clock etc.They are gateway numbers, based on 9 which is eternal trinity of trinities. Add any of the four numbers, then add the digits of the answer, and it will be one of the same numbers, they are indestructible and eternal. Multiply them in any combination, add the digits and the answer will be 9. For example:

$6 \times 9 = 54$ and $5 + 4 = 9$

$9 \times 12 = 108$ and $1 + 0 + 8 = 9$

These times have polarities. 3.00 p.m. is a solar positive time, 3.00 a.m. is lunar, a time when your energy is at its lowest. As a child I recorded the activities of Tomby the gnome who always emerged at these strong hours of the day.

I was planting lavender close to the stone when the big buzz began. It started as a subdued drone and rose to a monastic hum. The day was windless and there was only one bee visible, a bumble, and he was one octave higher than the humming which filled the garden. Within the hum were wave-like rhythms which brought gusts of perfume, rich incense of rosemary and peppermint and gorse flowers.

The big buzz came in closer, focussed itself into one vibrating air pocket next to the stone and changed to a pulsating silence. There was a smell of elder sap, and a little man appeared. He stood there solidly, his arms at his sides, and he was challenging me with eyes the colour of wood smoke.

'My name is Mohecan.' he announced, and his voice was remarkably human, deep and full of authority. He was only about 3 ft tall but he had a presence not to be argued with.

'Hello.'

He didn't want niceties.

'You are a giant' he said 'And I am the fairy medicine man, Mohecan. Heed what I shall tell you.'

I put down my trowel from where it had paused in mid-air, and gave Mohecan my full attention. He looked more human than a fairy, solid enough to touch in his square grey coat. He was bare-headed and bald, with a whiskery beard, and his wrinkled hands were the colour of rhubarb.They moved stiffly as if he was very very old. His feet were deep in the grass and partly covered by the coat.

Its grey colour was threaded with gold in a honeycomb pattern, and whether this was stitching or whether it was golden light was impossible to tell.

The Medicine Man Speaks

Next to my box of lavender plants, I sat spell bound while this dumpy little man talked with Shakespearian eloquence.

'I am Mohecan, the medicine man. I work with the fairies and I come to you in peace.

Five hundred and ninety years ago I raised this granite stone. Into each crystal have I whispered knowledge and each is programmed to release energy to those who open their hearts in the presence of this stone.

A circle of sage and mint, sweet banks of marjoram, lavender and thyme once surrounded this stone. The perfume and the song of bees created the spiritual essence of medicine and drew from the stone the harmonies of its note. I blended the fine vibrations of plant and crystal, and the two combined are very potent. This is fairy medicine. The nearest thing you have today is called homeopathy.

The knowledge I share with you now is held deep in the cosmic consciousness, it circulates through the golden net whose arteries span both worlds.

80

There are many links between the plant and mineral kingdoms, and how to extract the essence of each plant and imbue it with the music of a crystal is a long forgotten healing secret. No matter how you choose to use a plant, whether you eat it, infuse it, smell it, hold it or burn it, that plant heals you with its SONG.

Its fragrance, taste and colour reach out to all your senses, but its song is seldom heard. Listen from the spirit! You have clairaudience too.

Mohecan paused and looked at me imperiously.

'You giants' he said with a touch of contempt. 'Lumbering around the place all the time.You could do far more effective work if you sat still and used your spirit selves.'

For a moment we both watched a bumble bee zig-zagging across the lavender plants. Then he continued.

'If only you could hear the bees as we hear them, for the bee echoes the note of each flower, the bee sings seven times seven times seven. This music is beyond your hearing range. This is why the wild flower meadows and the herb gardens are so needed - the unheard, undreamed of orchestra of wind and insect and flower heals the aura of the earth, enfolding those beings who choose to share it.

Now I will share my fairy medicine with you. I give you seven herbs linked with seven crystals to create a healing garden. Bury the crystals underneath each plant, and do not grieve for them. Let go of these shining treasures and let them work among your plants.

Fairy Medicine

ROSE QUARTZ WITH SAGE for the kindness of purity. For bringing acceptance and tranquillity to an over active mind, and for healing the link between the emotional and the physical.

CLEAR QUARTZ WITH LAVENDER to give powerful protection from airborne germs of cosmic origin for which the immune system is unprepared.

AMETHYST WITH HYSSOP for freedom from fear. All those illnesses based on fear - and fairies have these too - such as cause great tension in the head, throat and chest will respond to the SONG of this musical combination.

TIGER'S EYE WITH GOLDEN MARJORAM protects the spirit from being too human. With its eternal bass note it clears materialism from the aura, banishes greed and heals abuse. It is important that the marjoram has golden leaves, for this vibration is a direct echo of the golden ray.

TURQUOISE WITH LEMON BALM (MELLISSA). A strange but potent combination.Its power is in its polarities for the two energies are very different. The SONG of this blend is for discovery, for personal growth and letting go of limitations.

AVENTURINE WITH THYME. You must use seven different varieties of thyme. There are seven ways of healing the heart. Send love into the aventurine crystal which is green, and use each thyme as your intuition tells you for these seven songs. Love and music, love and fragrance, love and colour, love and sunshine, love and water, love and earth, love and angels.

CITRINE WITH CHAMOMILE, for sleep and serenity. The golden crystal will bring to the herb the quality of creative dreaming, the ability to listen from the spirit. While the body slumbers, the soul opens its petals like a lotus and absorbs its needs from seven celestial suns, the sun of creation, the sun of wisdom, the sun of love, the sun of joy, the sun of harmony, the sun of forgiveness and the sun of peace.'

After this incredibly long speech, Mohecan's wood smoke eyes questioned mine as if seeking reassurance. Remembering Elbino's instructions, I quickly picked a green leaf and held it against my heart.

'I promise to remember it all, and share it.'

Mohecan looked relieved. He nodded, and spread out his rhubarb hands, to show palms which glowed with light. When he moved, the honeycomb sparkled in his coat, and spread wide across the garden, a golden web between us which flickered long after he had gone.

Epilogue

'What are you?' I asked the fairies.

Blank faces.

'Do you know what you are?'

'Do you know what YOU are?' They fired the question straight back to me.

'I am a radiant being of light trying to cope inside a human body' I replied, and there was a silence while they digested this information.

A group of fairies hovered around me, in a semi circle, weightless but still, shimmering as they considered my question. These were blue light fairies, forget-me-not blue and hazy. I had to keep de-focusing my eyes to see them, it was easier just to sense their moth-like presence.

'God is in us.'

The words came by telepathy, from the clearest fairy in the group, and as she spoke she was filled with a bright star. It quickly multiplied into a chain of stars which blazed so brightly that I had to look away. They rose like thistle seeds and drifted deep into the water plants until they were camouflaged by the glitters of the morning sun.

'God is in us. That is all you need to know.'

Of course it was all I needed to know. But my brain still quested for a longer explanation, (like brains do!) I tuned in to the spirit and asked about the fairies. These are the words I received.

'Fairies, as you call them, are part of the divine network of light which cradles this planet. They are born at the meeting points of energy lines, and they respond to you by manifesting in a form that is pleasing to you. They are not physical. But there are other life forms of the fairy kingdom, such as gnomes, who are closer to being physical than the star fairies. Gnomes have a lower vibration and slightly more density than fairies, so they are earth bound, closer to being human. The life which God created is based on music, and each life form has a different note spanning 3 octaves. You humans range between middle C and the A, five notes above, it is not by chance you use this note for tuning! It is your note! The fairies are at least an octave higher, some are so high their note would be beyond the hearing range of the human ear. Cats and birds are between you and the fairies, plants and rocks below. The deepest note, so deep it can only be felt, is in the heart of the earth, it is the note of the planet. Its vibration is spaced so wide that it resembles a heart beat. It can be experienced by powerful water falls. Listen and you will detect a rhythm deep in the falling water. Or it can be seen in the way a spring of water emerges from the earth - it bubbles up with a regular pulse.'

All life is interlaced with celestial light, and it has a geometric structure like that of a mystic rose. All that is beautiful is one, Art, music, mathematics, colour, light, crystals, all of them are networked with the love of the creator.

Fairies are not mentioned in the Bible, you say! Fairies twinkled in the sands of the holy land, and the salt of the seas, and the crystals on the Ark of the Covenant. Fairies networked in the vines and the fig trees, and in the cotton plants, spirits unseen. Points of light. Stars on the sea.

Fairies and angels are very close. You could say the fairies are diffusions of angel energy. What the fairies told you is true - if only you would just accept these simple truths.'

I was reminded of the words of John Keats.

'Beauty is truth, and truth beauty
That is all ye know on earth
and all ye need to know.'

FREE DETAILED CATALOGUE

Capall Bann is owned and run by people actively involved in many of the areas in which we publish. A detailed illustrated catalogue is available on request, SAE or International Postal Coupon appreciated. **Titles can be ordered direct from Capall Bann, post free in the UK** (cheque or PO with order) or from good bookshops and specialist outlets.
Do contact us for details on the latest releases at: **Capall Bann Publishing, Freshfields, Chieveley, Berks, RG20 8TF.** Titles include:

A Breath Behind Time, Terri Hector
Angels and Goddesses - Celtic Christianity & Paganism, M. Howard
Arthur - The Legend Unveiled, C Johnson & E Lung
Astrology The Inner Eye - A Guide in Everyday Language, E Smith
Auguries and Omens - The Magical Lore of Birds, Yvonne Aburrow
Asyniur - Womens Mysteries in the Northern Tradition, S McGrath
Beginnings - Geomancy, Builder's Rites & Electional Astrology in the
       European Tradition, Nigel Pennick
Between Earth and Sky, Julia Day
Book of the Veil , Peter Paddon
Caer Sidhe - Celtic Astrology and Astronomy, Vol 1, Michael Bayley
Caer Sidhe - Celtic Astrology and Astronomy, Vol 2 M Bayley
Call of the Horned Piper, Nigel Jackson
Cat's Company, Ann Walker
Celtic Faery Shamanism, Catrin James
Celtic Faery Shamanism - The Wisdom of the Otherworld, Catrin James
Celtic Lore & Druidic Ritual, Rhiannon Ryall
Celtic Sacrifice - Pre Christian Ritual & Religion, Marion Pearce
Celtic Saints and the Glastonbury Zodiac, Mary Caine
Circle and the Square, Jack Gale
Compleat Vampyre - The Vampyre Shaman, Nigel Jackson
Creating Form From the Mist - The Wisdom of Women in Celtic Myth and
       Culture, Lynne Sinclair-Wood
Crystal Clear - A Guide to Quartz Crystal, Jennifer Dent
Crystal Doorways, Simon & Sue Lilly
Crossing the Borderlines - Guising, Masking & Ritual Animal Disguise in the
       European Tradition, Nigel Pennick
Dragons of the West, Nigel Pennick
Earth Dance - A Year of Pagan Rituals, Jan Brodie
Earth Harmony - Places of Power, Holiness & Healing, Nigel Pennick

Earth Magic, Margaret McArthur
Eildon Tree (The) Romany Language & Lore, Michael Hoadley
Enchanted Forest - The Magical Lore of Trees, Yvonne Aburrow
Eternal Priestess, Sage Weston
Eternally Yours Faithfully, Roy Radford & Evelyn Gregory
Everything You Always Wanted To Know About Your Body, But So Far
    Nobody's Been Able To Tell You, Chris Thomas & D Baker
Face of the Deep - Healing Body & Soul, Penny Allen
Fairies in the Irish Tradition, Molly Gowen
Familiars - Animal Powers of Britain, Anna Franklin
Fool's First Steps, (The) Chris Thomas
Forest Paths - Tree Divination, Brian Harrison, Ill. S. Rouse
From Past to Future Life, Dr Roger Webber
Gardening For Wildlife Ron Wilson
God Year, The, Nigel Pennick & Helen Field
Goddess on the Cross, Dr George Young
Goddess Year, The, Nigel Pennick & Helen Field
Goddesses, Guardians & Groves, Jack Gale
Handbook For Pagan Healers, Liz Joan
Handbook of Fairies, Ronan Coghlan
Healing Book, The, Chris Thomas and Diane Baker
Healing Homes, Jennifer Dent
Healing Journeys, Paul Williamson
Healing Stones, Sue Philips
Herb Craft - Shamanic & Ritual Use of Herbs, Lavender & Franklin
Hidden Heritage - Exploring Ancient Essex, Terry Johnson
Hub of the Wheel, Skytoucher
In Search of Herne the Hunter, Eric Fitch
Inner Celtia, Alan Richardson & David Annwn
Inner Mysteries of the Goths, Nigel Pennick
Inner Space Workbook - Develop Thru Tarot, C Summers & J Vayne
Intuitive Journey, Ann Walker Isis - African Queen, Akkadia Ford
Journey Home, The, Chris Thomas
Kecks, Keddles & Kesh - Celtic Lang & The Cog Almanac, Bayley
Language of the Psycards, Berenice
Legend of Robin Hood, The, Richard Rutherford-Moore
Lid Off the Cauldron, Patricia Crowther
Light From the Shadows - Modern Traditional Witchcraft, Gwyn
Living Tarot, Ann Walker
Lore of the Sacred Horse, Marion Davies
Lost Lands & Sunken Cities (2nd ed.), Nigel Pennick
Magic of Herbs - A Complete Home Herbal, Rhiannon Ryall
Magical Guardians - Exploring the Spirit and Nature of Trees, Philip Heselton
Magical History of the Horse, Janet Farrar & Virginia Russell
Magical Lore of Animals, Yvonne Aburrow
Magical Lore of Cats, Marion Davies

Magical Lore of Herbs, Marion Davies
Magick Without Peers, Ariadne Rainbird & David Rankine
Masks of Misrule - Horned God & His Cult in Europe, Nigel Jackson
Medicine For The Coming Age, Lisa Sand MD
Medium Rare - Reminiscences of a Clairvoyant, Muriel Renard
Menopausal Woman on the Run, Jaki da Costa
Mind Massage - 60 Creative Visualisations, Marlene Maundrill
Mirrors of Magic - Evoking the Spirit of the Dewponds, P Heselton
Moon Mysteries, Jan Brodie
Mysteries of the Runes, Michael Howard
Mystic Life of Animals, Ann Walker
New Celtic Oracle The, Nigel Pennick & Nigel Jackson
Oracle of Geomancy, Nigel Pennick
Pagan Feasts - Seasonal Food for the 8 Festivals, Franklin & Phillips
Patchwork of Magic - Living in a Pagan World, Julia Day
Pathworking - A Practical Book of Guided Meditations, Pete Jennings
Personal Power, Anna Franklin
Pickingill Papers - The Origins of Gardnerian Wicca, Bill Liddell
Pillars of Tubal Cain, Nigel Jackson
Places of Pilgrimage and Healing, Adrian Cooper
Practical Divining, Richard Foord
Practical Meditation, Steve Hounsome
Practical Spirituality, Steve Hounsome
Psychic Self Defence - Real Solutions, Jan Brodie
Real Fairies, David Tame
Reality - How It Works & Why It Mostly Doesn't, Rik Dent
Romany Tapestry, Michael Houghton
Runic Astrology, Nigel Pennick
Sacred Animals, Gordon MacLellan
Sacred Celtic Animals, Marion Davies, Ill. Simon Rouse
Sacred Dorset - On the Path of the Dragon, Peter Knight
Sacred Grove - The Mysteries of the Forest, Yvonne Aburrow
Sacred Geometry, Nigel Pennick
Sacred Nature, Ancient Wisdom & Modern Meanings, A Cooper
Sacred Ring - Pagan Origins of British Folk Festivals, M. Howard
Season of Sorcery - On Becoming a Wisewoman, Poppy Palin
Seasonal Magic - Diary of a Village Witch, Paddy Slade
Secret Places of the Goddess, Philip Heselton
Secret Signs & Sigils, Nigel Pennick
Self Enlightenment, Mayan O'Brien
Spirits of the Air, Jaq D Hawkins
Spirits of the Earth, Jaq D Hawkins
Spirits of the Earth, Jaq D Hawkins
Stony Gaze, Investigating Celtic Heads John Billingsley
Stumbling Through the Undergrowth , Mark Kirwan-Heyhoe
Subterranean Kingdom, The, revised 2nd ed, Nigel Pennick

Symbols of Ancient Gods, Rhiannon Ryall
Talking to the Earth, Gordon MacLellan
Taming the Wolf - Full Moon Meditations, Steve Hounsome
Teachings of the Wisewomen, Rhiannon Ryall
The Other Kingdoms Speak, Helena Hawley
Tree: Essence of Healing, Simon & Sue Lilly
Tree: Essence, Spirit & Teacher, Simon & Sue Lilly
Through the Veil, Peter Paddon
Torch and the Spear, Patrick Regan
Understanding Chaos Magic, Jaq D Hawkins
Vortex - The End of History, Mary Russell
Warp and Weft - In Search of the I-Ching, William de Fancourt
Warriors at the Edge of Time, Jan Fry
Water Witches, Tony Steele
Way of the Magus, Michael Howard
Weaving a Web of Magic, Rhiannon Ryall
West Country Wicca, Rhiannon Ryall
Wildwitch - The Craft of the Natural Psychic, Poppy Palin
Wildwood King , Philip Kane
Witches of Oz, Matthew & Julia Philips
Wondrous Land - The Faery Faith of Ireland by Dr Kay Mullin
Working With the Merlin, Geoff Hughes
Your Talking Pet, Ann Walker

FREE detailed catalogue and FREE 'Inspiration' magazine

Contact: Capall Bann Publishing, Freshfields, Chieveley, Berks, RG20 8TF